JED PASCOE'S
THE FUNNY SIDE OF 60s

Published in the UK by
POWERFRESH Limited
Unit 3 Everdon Park
Heartlands Industrial Estate
Daventry
NN11 5YJ

Telephone + 44 01327 871 777
Facsimile + 44 01327 879 222
E.Mail info@powerfresh.co.uk

ISBN 1874125252

Printed in the UK by Belmont Press
Powerfresh Reprint September 2004

OCCUPATIONS FOR THE RETIRED

NO.1 MERCHANT BANKER

OCCUPATIONS FOR THE RETIRED

No. **2** HAIRDRESSER

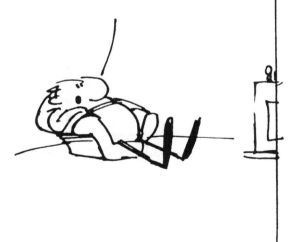

OCCUPATIONS FOR THE RETIRED

NO.3 SOLICITOR

OCCUPATIONS FOR THE RETIRED

No.4 POLICEMAN

OCCUPATIONS FOR THE RETIRED

No.5 SURGEON

No. 6 ARCHITECT

No 9   FASHION DESIGNER

No.10 ESTATE AGENT

OCCUPATIONS FOR THE RETIRED

No. 11 AIRLINE PILOT

No. 12 CIVIL ENGINEERING
CONTRACTOR

OCCUPATIONS FOR THE RETIRED

No. 13 SUBMARINE COMMANDER

No 14 MARKETING DIRECTOR

OCCUPATIONS FOR THE RETIRED

No 15   DENTIST

JED PASCOE
NATIONAL AND INTERNATIONAL
AWARD WINNING
CARTOONIST.
LIVING PROOF THAT
EMPTY VESSELS MAKE
MOST NOISE..
TOTALLY CONFUSED BY
LIFE, HE LIVES MAINLY
IN HIS BELEAGURED
IMAGINATION — WHICH
IS ENOUGH TO
CONFUSE ANYONE. AND
STILL LOOKING FOR FAME
AND FORTUNE, IF ANYONE
OUT THERE IS INTERESTED.